LUCK

Also by Marc Elihu Hofstadter

House of Peace
Visions
Shark's Tooth

LUCK

POEMS

MARC ELIHU HOFSTADTER

Scarlet Tanager
BOOKS

Cover photo by Jason Coyne http://jasoncoyne.smugmug.com
The image is of a Roman 2nd century A.D. copy of a
Greek 4th century B.C. statue of Apollo attributed to
Praxiteles. Louvre, Paris.
Author photo by Mayona Engdahl
Cover and page design, and composition by Dickie Magidoff

Published by:
Scarlet Tanager Books
P.O. Box 20906
Oakland, CA 94620
www.scarlettanager.com

Library of Congress Cataloging-in-Publication Data

Hofstadter, Marc Elihu, 1945-
  Luck : poems / by Marc Elihu Hofstadter.
    p. cm.
  ISBN 978-0-9768676-1-6 (alk. paper)
  I. Title.
  PS3608.O48L83 2008
  811'.6--dc22
                                        2008034180

Acknowledgments

Grateful acknowledgment is made to the editors of the following publications in which these works or earlier versions of them previously appeared:

Cadillac Cicatrix: "Tower of Babel"

California Quarterly: "Particulars"

California State Poetry Society Poetry Letter and Literary Review: "Israeli Cockroaches"

Cape Rock: "Son House"

Controlled Burn: "Fortunate"

descant: "The Rational Man," "Sea Bass"

Evansville Review: "San Francisco Evening"

Griffin: "Provincetown Painter"

Meridian Anthology of Contemporary Poetry: "Keep On"

/nor: "Growth"

PKA's Advocate: "Manya and Albert," "The Return"

Poetry International: "Not Yours"

Redwood Coast Review: "Multiplicity," "My Religion," "Silver Lake, 1970," "Stars"

River Oak Review: "Orléans"

RiverSedge: "Guggenheim Museum"

Ship of Fools: "Côte-d'Or Visit"

Southern Indiana Review: "Young Man"

Street Sheet: "Old Man Smoking"

Texas Review: "Baths"

My "bag of miscellaneous spices" ("Particulars," page 47) has mingled with the "mist, pollen, and fireplace smoke" of the following people to produce this book:

my unparalleled teachers: Alfred Levinson, David Mus, Frédéric J. Grover, Samuel Hynes, Clive Matson, Kim Addonizio, Mark Wunderlich, Sarah Rosenthal, Marcia Falk, Christopher Hewitt;

that unparalleled poet and philosopher Yves Bonnefoy, whose friendship I cherish;

my unparalleled friend and mentor the poet, translator, anthologist and scholar Willis Barnstone, who suggested the title of this book;

that unparalleled spiritual guide Vince Morgante;

those unparalleled poet/critics who read and commented on this manuscript: Yvonne Cannon, Leonard J. Cirino, Patricia Edith, Dian Gillmar, Gloria Grover, Ernie Karsten, Stephen Kessler, Jeanne Lupton, Daniel Marlin, Janell Moon, Elaine Starkman, Jan Steckel;

my unparalleled writing colleagues Paul Belz, Maureen Crisick, Jannie Dresser, Jane Falk, Dale Jensen, Judy Wells, Mitchell Zeftel;

my unparalleled friends Firdosh and Carla Anklesaria, Donald Caplin, Mayona Engdahl, Nicholas Follansbee, Judith Ginsberg, Claire Grover, Colin Guiver, Prudence Hall, Les Kong, Ruth Korn, Sandra Rappy, Donald Sackheim, Mark Sherkow, Peter Straus, Tom Usher, Tom Wagstaff;

and the one who defines the meaning of the word "unparalleled" for me: David Zurlin.

Contents

Full and Empty Places

Addressed to You

Making Love

For David Zurlin

Not Yours

Not Yours

Some days nothing is yours.
Not the bed you sleep in,
your favorite Paisley shirt,
or even the sky,
speckled with cold white.
Your partner's tone carefully reminds you
he's his own man,
and your friends maintain
an adult distance.
You're not even master of yourself:
your moods run off in zigzag rivulets,
like spilled milk.
Nothing to do but wait it out,
try to sit emptied of thought
until the world in its own sweet time
floods back—
for your life wasn't given to you,
only lent,
and one day you're going to have to give it back.

Breeze in the Branches

Don't ask for more than a breeze in the branches.
Don't expect the sun to imprint a brassy crown
on your naked skull, the midnight moon
to last all morning, the oriole
to perch on your finger for human food.
Light blooms until its petals collapse to the soil.
So, your heart.
Try to imprison stars in a cage,
the sea in a stone,
you'll fail.
Release the creature
trapped in your clenched fist,
let it go.

My Religion

Black sky's awhirl with stars.
I'm young, afraid of everything.
I fall to my knees in the cloistered plaza,
in the thick forest, on our front lawn,
and swoon at the sight of so many
fires blazing in such vast space.
Kneeling, I pray to the myriad lights,
the vault, whatever it is holding all this
so far above my jellied eyes,
until I'm just one more small fire
sending out my tiny spark of light.

Barrel

When my copy of Yeats' *Collected Poems*
with the arabesqued blue-and-white dust jacket
sprouted spongy mold along its edges, I gave up
what hope I ever had of having things
the way I wanted them. I'm sixty now:
my thighs hurt, my knowledge
is limited to certain books I've read,
my diet's only good as my last meal.
What branch is tendered to my hand to grasp?
Nothing but this present moment, this,
and then another one, with only, perhaps,
hope crouching at the bottom of the barrel.

Rainy Afternoon

It's raining
and the dead turn slowly head over heels
in the warm sea.
They will never see the sun again.
Never glimpse another naked body.
They will feel only the anemone's kiss,
watch the lonely weave of the seahorse.
It rains and rains,
but the dead don't notice.
Only we, with our lamps burning, feel the chill.

Fortunate

What a stroke of luck that buttered toast
tastes slightly salty, that the crack of a baseball
bat in April wakes one up to life,
that I met you through an otherwise
stupid dating service, that my parents
hit it off all those years ago
at the Ittelsons' musical evening,
that someone once thought up the Big Bang,
and that my cat Willie,
who died ten years ago,
loved to rub his side against my pants,
grateful for their electric warmth.

Jaunty Stroll

I don't understand what's happening:
what are these rays filling streets
with iridescent fenders, crowding sidewalks
with Technicolor gazes? No particular
o'clock in the morning but things
have been shining for a while
and will go on hours more
whether I'm here or not but I'm
this locus of sight and smell
swinging arms as it strolls
jauntily past dogs and strollers
knowing somehow how to place
foot after foot and breathe scents
of plum blossom and magnolia.

The Rational Man

I am the blossom of all I hate.
In me the sensible man annuls
dreams of Orpheus or Ra.
The scientist in my cerebrum
divides the world into suns and stones.
The New Critic residing in my gut
sees the poem as a word machine.
In me the whole of Skepticism
raises itself on its heroic elbow
and looks down condescendingly
on everything holy.

Waving Branches

I was fifteen the first time I experienced God. Bob Eubank and I wandered in woods near Larchmont, New York. As a mighty breeze made maple, dogwood, and spruce branches shake their scents into our nostrils, I became aware of Him looking out of each trembling branch, twig, and leaf, each unbelievably green fern, each pebble pressing into my bare feet. His voice was in the screaming blue jays, the whining gnats, the swift-scudding clouds. Dust motes in the air danced and shimmered, his angels.

Twenty years later, I sat on a wooden bench in a dusty Jerusalem park reading when I raised my head almost involuntarily to see dark oak branches waving in bright light, which seemed to be signaling me as it flashed on and off. My chest puffed out, my fingers tingled, my pulse throbbed violently, my brain was penetrated by light. "What's happening?" I cried, and immediately found myself sitting on the hard bench, the small, faint type of my book before my eyes.

Ten years later, I attended my father's funeral in a little Jewish cemetery in Santa Cruz. As the rabbi intoned a mournful Hebrew song to the group huddled around the fresh grave, I looked up to see branches of the enormous eucalyptus trees surrounding the site slowly, silently waving. With my father dead, I felt as though part of me was already on the other side. It was on that side, I saw, that these sickle-shaped, gray leaves were clattering against one another, but too high for me to hear.

Stained

An oily smudge spoiling
the pristine page of poetry
rankles me so much
it seems to grow and grow,
swallowing first the page,
then the book, the room,
the sky, and finally
the whole world, at which point
I have no choice
but to accept it.

Meal for the Starving

Does a boy with pus streaming
from gummy eyes love God?
Should he be grateful that he
can breathe sultry air, savor
gruel's gritty texture?
He smiles for a moment at
his loving, scrawny, fearful mother,
wonders if she questions God
too. Then he starts to think
about his next meal, a long
twenty-four hours away.
He steels himself against the dark time
of disbelief, knowing he'll
thrill to the food again when
it's placed before his eager,
questioning gaze.

Reading Poetry

When I was ten, eleven,
I would read poems—
Frost, Sandburg, Amy Lowell—
and understand little
but get a vague, dreamy feeling
on which I'd float
like a twig on a summer stream.
Now, over sixty,
many poems and poets
under my belt, I read
critically, carefully,
but sometimes come across
a line from which I get a
vague, dreamy feeling
on which I float . . .

Tea Bar

I lounge in a tea bar
as on so many other afternoons.
Time, continuous,
ignores our day, night, day.

We parcel it out like a row of teas to be tasted—
Darjeeling Second Flush, Assam, Nilgiri—
labels put on tastes and colors, soil types and rainfalls,
but all actually from the same bush.

The afternoon streams along
from some inexhaustible source,
carrying us all together
on a boat down a broad river:

well-dressed couple leaning close,
green-haired girl with nose-ring,
elderly women lifting pinkies,
teenaged boy with headphones.

The sun tinkles on blue and brown teapots,
green and amber liquids,
teaspoons and forks.
Traffic noise buzzes through the door,

sycamores wave outside,
catchy reggae's on the stereo.
Where are we headed?
Who knows?

We sip our Pu-Ehr, Silver Needles, Dragonwell
labeling our adventures
so as not to be too scared
of the blazing light.

Multiplicity

Six kinds of warbler dot my lawn,
my library's stocked with philosophies
of art and beauty,
last night I dreamed of Danes, croissants,
beagles, and palm trees,
my grandfather saw the world
through Torah, Yiddish slang,
and fear of Cossacks,
the roster of the Oakland A's
is revamped every year,
there's no end to arguments
about the benefits of globalization,
Americans are patriotic
while Spaniards swear by Spain,
the sky has millions of black holes
that may lead to other universes . . .
Do you think, when I die,
I will be granted even a capsule of truth,
or will it be just another moment
in an endless sequence
stretching from Big Bang
to who knows what?

The Fly

You alight on the toilet paper roll.
Tempted to swat you out of the world,
I hesitate, then look close.
Your head's an intricate, armored helmet,
your violet wings iridescent as a Dior,
your eyes so big they must see something.
Surely God squanders his genius on you:
you'll probably die today,
buzzing against my window.
Yet you breathe like I do,
see the world with an astonished gaze,
fight to reach the light.
I trap you in a jar and free you
into the front yard, wondering what you'll do
with this wide, clear day.

Living Low

Bury yourself beneath the grass.
Become small as a burrowing mole,
quiet as a worm filtering dirt.
Expect no more than the rich smell of clay.
Move slowly, wait patiently—
you can't ever possess the field,
only your quarter yard of loam and roots,
some moisture, a hint of air,
as the meadow flowers above you.

Threshold

The books are all lined up,
Addonizio to Zukovsky.
The pepper shaker's
full of darkness.
Lightning scalds the window
nuclear yellow.
My shoes point pointedly
at the door.
Everything is ready.

Autumn Rain

Thank you.
It's about time.
No more of that egg-yolk sun stuff.
Gray, leaden droplets pound the patio
and drench the rose.
I open my soul
to whatever beats me down,
deposits darkness in me,
engages me in sobriety, sadness, and surrender.
I stretch my arms to embrace
every black thing out there
that mirrors the hole within.

Stars

Massive blazes consume
hydrogen and helium
in endless, empty black,
clustering, colliding,
exploding to forge carbon,
iron, and lives like mine,
spinning, stretching over
vast space, burning
and burning and burning . . .
Is this the story we tell?
Are these the lamps we've hung
to light our trail?
Isn't there at the end
some floodlit stage
onto which we disembark
to applause and acclaim
and the mouths of loved ones
murmuring our names?

Does Size Matter?

How big is the universe?
What if it's infinite:
is that too big?
Can you stuff that in your pipe
and smoke it?
Or would you prefer
a smaller world,
one you can stretch your mind around
even if it hurts your straining neurons?
Me, I like it big and fearsome,
like some brawny jock
who could hold me up
and have his way with me,
filling me mightily
the way the universe fills us daily
with its pulsing strength.

Silver Lake, 1970

There I sprawled on cold, bare ground
gazing at a gazillion stars in chilled,
clean air, the scent of Silver Lake,
damp moss, and pine sap in my
nostrils, my ears buzzing with the
huge silence—
These memories are faint
as I pace city streets, read my library
books, say I believe in God or don't
believe. What would it take to look up
into immensity again, expand into space,
blaze like a star before my fire goes out?

You

Oh utter word that roots at the heart of the world,
let me see! I'm a worm rodent beast
who gazes up at your indistinguishable face
with all the ecstasy of humiliating death
I'm your servant child brother who obeys your commands
here in beds bookstores offices You screw me
like an overpowering ardent lover I submit
I've known you forever and don't know you at all
You set the great cymbals crashing the lightning
forking that illuminates the narrow path
through vines fronds savage blossoms
and the cities littered with rubbish and bodies
You don't explain You gaze with burning eyes
over the desert of my fate You live in
Blake St. John of the Cross Rimbaud you charge
electric tongues with the death roar of your infinite mercy
Drug visions seizures shudders are the convulsions
of your breast upon which men like me founder
Ultimate orgasm of the seas throw me foaming at the mouth
and ejaculating into the spume Rock me in your
nursing arms Show me how to thread my way
infinitesimal frightened unsure into this endless roar
Oh ultimate, I name you God Tao Spirit
I don't know what to call you You have
been with me from the beginning I am with you
beyond all ends Carry me into the valley
Hold me in the calm lake of your dream
Make me whole with your fierce grip

Days and Years

New York City Trash-Talk

I drew bus exhaust into my lungs
with pleasure, thinking it more real
than anything else I knew,
loved the garbage strewn
in Broadway gutters mixed
with smutty snow and ice
to congeal into pungent pudding.
I gazed delighted at the millions of starlings,
black, aggressive, who'd mass
above the West Side Highway
at dusk, dirtying the sky
with their thick bodies.
And the rough, brown-skinned boys,
pants tight, shirts ripped,
who'd pass me on 96th Street,
eyes bold and dangerous,
arms swinging like the wind
threatening to throw into my face
thrilling bits of trash:
chewed gum,
tobacco butts,
spit from wet, dark mouths.

My Big Sur

in memory of Robinson Jeffers

New York crowds surge shouting through Broadway
like waves slapping through a river channel.
High-cheekboned, Roman-nosed, thin- and thick-lipped
mingle like curlews, sandpipers, gulls on a beach.
Massive skyscrapers zoom up,
great granite cliffs puncturing the sky.
As fishing boats drag night nets,
so great-jawed trucks trawl Eighth Avenue at 3:00 AM
trapping Pepsi cans, condoms, used paperbacks.
And if I stand at the top of the Empire State
and survey the great, breathing Leviathan
laid out before me—sprinting streets,
scurrying pedestrians, rising vapors—
I see the same God you glimpse
when the breakers roar and the gray gulls scream
above the inhuman, multi-veined, many-towered sea.

22 Crescent Road

for Don Sackheim

Don and I want to steal a bit
of the past back, so drive to view
22 Crescent Road, its red brick
facade and stucco trim exactly the same
as fifty years ago, the maple
trees still littering winged seeds, the
yellow Mercury parked in the driveway
of our memory. I snap photos,
Don eggs me on, until cops arrive
and ask what the hell we're doing.
Apparently whoever lives in my house
doesn't want me there, is willing
to have me arrested for trying to preserve
the window from which I once gazed
with innocent eyes at a world of
chipmunks, petunias, and ravishing sun.

The Hot Corner

I was a "shrimp," but played third base
because of my strong arm. I dreamed
of hitting home runs like Mickey Mantle,
but couldn't drive it past shortstop.
My card collection included Mays, Aaron, Spahn;
I loved the wrappers' bubble-gum smell.
My talk was laced with references
to stances, strikes, change-ups.
Did anything else in the world exist?
What else was required beyond
the odor of fresh infield grass,
the rush of wind as I pursued a ball,
my heart pumping as though it would never stop?

Minor Nights

was what I called them as a child,
musical mode I thought captured
hours of moonlight and cool pillows
when oboes could almost be heard
silvering the blackened streets.
Not tragic, no, but bittersweet,
mixing notes of bright and dim:
melodies I preferred to major ones,
to brassy Handelian fanfares
or extroverted strings—
minor, since my life
was like that.

Blaze

I grasped the manes, stroked the soft necks,
whispered endearments into the nervous ears:
no horse could resist me.
Child though I was, I tamed the pinto
no one else could ride, marched it proudly
down the festooned street of my home town
in the Fourth of July parade.
In summer camp I adopted Zorro,
black gelding whose quick, bumpy
gallop pleased me. One day a counselor
who disliked me put me on Blaze,
gray, dappled filly, whose long, loping
strides threw me. I rolled over to avoid
being trampled by the horse behind,
dusted off my chinos, walked the mile
back to camp, never mounted
one of my beloveds again.

Lyra

We made out madly in the back row
of the movie theater in summer camp
all those years ago. You sat on my lap
as our tongues danced in one another's mouths
like butterflies in blossoms.
But when I went home and stupidly told my parents
about it, they flipped, called the camp
"immoral," kept me in sight for years,
teaching me such things are wrong and tawdry,
an approach my body believes in to this day.

Baths

Baths were my momma.
It's a wonder my skin didn't slough off.
I'd soak for hours,
not caring who I was, or why.
At eight I watched my penis float
like a lotus on the sudsy surface
while dreaming of flying across the Atlantic.
At sixteen I finished *Look Homeward, Angel*
in the tub, the pages growing damp,
the steamy water passionate as Eugene.
At college Tim took baths, too,
and I longed to share one with him,
his pale green eyes and upturned nose.
In grad school Larry A. nearly caught me
masturbating in the tub, truly in hot water,
but I hid myself behind cupped hands.
In my thirties I'd relax in the warmth,
delaying and delaying the long commute to work.
Now I take showers, my life rapider, busier.
But oh, for the heat of yesterday,
long evenings of immersion!

Concord, New Hampshire

Snow piled heavily against the clapboards
as we listened to *Tristan* over eggnog
and muffins. Vacationing with friends
and the boy I loved at the house of Ann's
parents, the living room was always filled
with people, the dining room with
turkey, cider, Christmas cookies.
He was dark, broad-shouldered, brown-
eyed, and read me passages from
Joyce and Durrell, tapping me on the
knee to stress key words. His sweat
mixed with the eggnog and moldy
books. And he didn't love me.

Black Angel

I was the "Black Angel of Death,"
soaring Air Canada from B.C. to S.F.,
my reign to end with the merge
into "Love's Body," where we'd all be one.
My parents met me at the airport,
committed me to a locked ward;
I was fed Thorazine and Stelazine.
When I wasn't killed there,
I reconsidered my philosophy.
But frightened my love of men,
reason for all the paranoia,
would be discovered, I hid it
from myself as well as them.
So much suffering
from being who I wasn't.
Thirty-five years later
how could it have ended otherwise
than a fall into "normalcy,"
savoring men and writing poems?

Typing Pool

Twelve of us, eleven women and I,
leaned into hulking Royal manuals,
tapping out affidavits, five-year plans,
letters, seven carbons to a page,
slopping whiteout on each sheet
when things went wrong.
Dolores complained of a stomach hernia,
failing eyesight, anxiety. Stella's
long face never broadened to a smile.
Eva chain-smoked and criticized
Dolores. Darlene was cute, efficient,
clearly there only for a year or two.
Then there was Helen—fat,
wall-eyed, the Buddha
around whom this circus whirled.
When I had problems I went to her.
Desperate to be back in school, sick
of following line after ant-trail line,
I'd drink Helen's comfort down
like an elixir. After a year I left for good.
I wonder how many of them
are still there, hunched in front of
blinding monitors, deleting,
inserting, cutting and pasting.

Orléans

Narrow treeless streets the cathedral lacy
as a wedding cake the Café de la Chancellerie's
madeleines and bitter coffee the bookstore's
paperbacks the color of cream the tulip
marigold calla lily beds replanted
by the municipality every other week
around the equestrian statue of Joan of Arc
Madame Ramon selling leeks and mandarin
oranges discussing the weather every day
as I made my rounds with my string bag
Au Petit Duc's chocolate porcupines
and quince tarts the old woman across the way
from us toiling in her kitchen as we savored
hot baguettes at 7 AM the Floral Park's
irises and flamingoes the bus ride
to the university across the Loire
raindrops or snowflakes dimpling its opaque
surface the outskirts dense with rose farms
where are you now Orléans of course
you're still there it's I who am missing

Kibbutz Mizra

was too hot to be idyllic.
I'd never seen a place so dusty.
We woke at 4 AM
to harvest crisp, green pears,
napped from noon till 3.
The earth beneath my feet
walking to the swimming pool
was dry as the Dead Sea Scrolls.
One day I ventured out across
the brown, savage fields to find,
at the edge of the unpaved highway,
a food stand—chocolates, gum
drops, icy Cokes—and brought them
back to the shack (where cockroaches
flew through the air and the radio
droned incomprehensible lyrics)
to devour big bites of chocolate,
down great gulps of soda.

Israeli Cockroaches

were five inches long, fluttered
from curtain to curtain like birds,
and stared with intelligent, dog-like eyes.
When one brushed my cheek in the
kibbutz cabin, I screamed.
Another time, Jill lifted
the sugar bowl lid in a Haifa hotel
and one lay there, filling
the whole thing with its black bulk.
Or there was the day our apartment manager
in Jerusalem squished four with his foot,
the juice staining the floor,
as he proclaimed, "No problem!"
I miss them, for if I never see them again,
I'll also never see the squat walls
of the Old City, never hear
the billion-voiced bird chorus
of the Jezreel Valley, never smell
the fresh vapor of the Kinneret.

Jerusalem

You are magenta thistles,
rose light on yellow stone,
men in black frowning their way
across cobblestones.
I'm far from you
among multiplexes,
hamburger joints,
women with Chevies
and three blond kids.
It's been thirty years.
Send me a fistful
of your torrid sunbeams,
roll me six falafel balls
to crunch my teeth on,
remember the one
who loved you
and left you behind!

New Year's Day, 1982

Faint light, thin
air of first day
of new year.
A lot has happened—

more will?
A year
of illness, nearly
demise,

but now, feeling
the chill
outside,
warmth in this

café where
tired faces drink
tea and wine,
smoke curls

up to oak rafters,
sun slants
through windows,
prism-like.

I have come through
like the light
that warms faces,
sets eyes aglow,

wan,
persistent,
slicing up
the cold.

Funeral

Gray eucalypti sway, clattering above
while the rabbi intones a Hebrew prayer.
I try to grasp something
that hovers above the polyurethane box of ashes,
the mourners huddled, moaning grief.
I almost hear it in the eloquent Kaddish.
My father suffered,
but his dying was quick.
Did he glimpse the thing at the last moment?
Can I clasp it between the lines of prayer?
I know only what I can't take in
in the soughing breeze,
the rabbi's minor-key songs,
the open grave with red dirt piled near.
Then the service is over.
We file onto suburban pavement,
eat corned beef at my mother's house.

Newly Retired

Now I'm one of those who sit,
thumbs worrying knuckles,
on park benches, waiting for something
to appear at our feet
and cure us of our dilemma
of too many hours, too little time.
Like kids, we crack jokes,
pull each others' sleeves,
reduced to pranks and tricks,
but we're utterly serious about our losses.
It seems we've been this way forever,
but we're surprised as you
at our thin arms and wattled throats.
Yet we're strong enough to hold on
as the wind jerks our branch around,
passionate enough to blurt "I love you"
to a grandson come to drive us home.

Growth

This skin-tag on my left thigh appeared
overnight, and proves I will die
as surely as an obit with a date on it.
Not soon, necessarily, but age is age
and this elongated, pinkish flap's
a flag trumpeting time's decay.
But what's my choice? Cut it off
for it to grow back again,
or try to love it as one does
an awkward grandchild or palsied neighbor?
As long as it lives, so do I.
We grow together, it blindly persisting,
I trying to be adult
and cherish all that stems from me,
the life I lead without choosing it day by day.
And so I can almost embrace
this funny-looking thing.

Whooping Cough

It comes out of you without your consent—
whoop, whoop, whoop as you gasp for breath—
and you wish it away, but it's in you,
has chosen you as its host for months,
its body to fester in, its cellar to mildew,
until you're almost used to cough and spit:
that's who you are now, the one who coughs,
whoop, whoop, whoop,
savage music of the windpipe and throat
that rings throughout your house
having taken you over, your master,
not caring if you're happy or not,
if you live or die,
until it seems part of you forever,
that even at the moment of death
you will think of nothing,
have no revelation, only insanely repeat,
whoop, whoop, whoop.

Particulars

How strange that I've done just what I have:
ridden cane-seated New York City streetcars,
burned piles of piquant fall Westchester leaves,
kissed a girl for the first time by the banks of the Crum
at midnight, smoked dope and gone nuts
in hippie-kingdom Santa Cruz, done the shopping
rounds of Orléans with my string bag,
drunk Turkish coffee with Arabs in the Old City
of Jerusalem, wandered feverish with HIV
through the sex-crazed Castro, moved here
in luxurious seclusion with the love
of my life, and now lie in bed drinking Assam tea
reading the poetry of Hayden Carruth—
it's all been so particular, so specific,
I can't think of a reason for any of it,
except perhaps that this is what
each of us is: a bag of miscellaneous
spices that trembles in the ambient breeze,
our unique odors carried to our neighbors' houses
where they mix with mist, pollen, and fireplace smoke.

Full and Empty Places

Old Man

for Prudence Hall

I strode there once where live oaks
scratched the sky and indigo lakes
trembled with light, trod loamy paths
past fern, moss and lichen, heard
deer rustle in the bushes, rose high
over forest, cliff, and creek
to breathe the freshness of the mist,
built a fire and heated beef, ate
with my hands, and drank river water
clear as diamonds, and made love to you
under a billion stars watched by the
old man in the mountain who made
all this and can destroy it—I walked
there, but no more, stuck in the
city, breathing smoke, hearing a rough
anvil clang and clang—while my living ghost
dwells there in peak, lake, and rock,
and loves the old man of the mountain,
his craggy, jagged profile.

San Francisco Evening

The old, peeling balcony of my
dinner host is dewy underfoot
and sways as I step, precariously,
like a vintage wine slightly shaken.
I could easily jump or fall onto the lawn
thirty feet below, but don't.
I leave the savory pot roast,
sweet, pink new potatoes,
buttered Brussels sprouts,
the conversation of friends,
and venture out to place fingers
on the cool, moist railing,
savor the misty, pollen-scented air,
and gaze at city lights—
a hundred windows nearby,
some framing dark, moving heads—
and at the black, silent skyscrapers downtown
and the fairy-tale lights on the bridge and water
(where boats glide slowly,
no doubt, in the stillness),
and across the bay to Oakland and Berkeley
where people live other lives,
their dinners perhaps also over,
and I wonder if some venture
onto their balconies
to observe lights and buildings,
bridge and windows,
to feel they could fall, yet don't,
in this evening that carries us aloft
like an ocean liner
coasting through filmy half-light.

Darjeeling Spring

Afternoon sun turns the teahouse window gold.
Cell phones tinkle, one man regales another
with rock climb tales, a dark-skinned woman
ripples her hips, and philodendron tendrils wave
like friends. My First Flush Darjeeling tastes
as spring-like as its little leaves are green.
Miniature dancers *pas de deux* in my brain.
I know the light will later turn so oblique
it will miss this room. My tea will grow cold.
People will leave to sauté onions and beef.
So I pay attention to each remark I overhear,
every muscled arm and swelling breast,
looks that gleam in nine directions,
mingled clinks, coughs, and chuckles,
until it all seems orchestrated by a brilliant composer,
its meaning a song without words.

Sophia Café, Albany, California

for Jane Falk

We munch on latkes and swill mint tea
as the place fills with men in yarmulkes
and women wearing shawls. Throngs of boys with payes
and girls sporting long socks run, squeal, and shriek.
I recall the dinners with my parents, uncles, cousins
in which we shared borscht, gefilte fish, Manischewitz.
You and I, friends since childhood,
debate the qualities of a mysterious, ineffable God.
I say, If He's unknowable, how do we know He exists?
I shake hands with the waiter, Avi, twenty and gray-eyed,
who tells me he considers food God's blessing.
People raise their voices in raucous laughter
and enjoyment of knishes, cholent, kneidlach,
which have kept our people persisting, flourishing
in scholarship, piety, and poetry for centuries.
We let the waves of conversation wash over us.
Maybe I'm not quite a believer, but these black, curly beards,
boisterous accents, charming children, tasty foods,
and general commotion make God seem, this evening,
a little more knowable.

Sea Bass

Tiny candlelit bistro—
grainy oak walls,
quirky radio jazz,
window steaming up
in spattering fall rain,
sea bass and broccoli
on a bed of rice
served by a cordial waitress.
What if life consisted
of charming, manageable days,
catchy rhythms,
morsels?

In a Music Store

Salif Keita acts neighborly with Brel
and Matti Caspi. Up ahead Miles
blows blue alongside Bix
and modest Lester, while down the aisle
Bob Dylan nasally insists. I stroll
to where *Brandenburg Concertos,*
Fidelio, La Mer stretch what seems
a half mile dancing with various
sonatas, motets, *lieder,* suites.
Then there are all the trombonists
I don't know, the salsa singers, obscure
nineteenth-century symphonists,
rock groups less famous than
the Stones or Kinks, polka troupes,
sitar players—millions of horn blasts,
guitar strums, drum beats chorusing together.
I whirl and spin until the stereo
plays a tune by Fauré I love
and I focus intently on its single lament.

Guggenheim Museum

Though not a believer,
I did have a cathedral
that bloomed on Fifth Avenue,
dome soaring
over vast vault,
Kandinskys and Klees
emblazoning the spiral walkway
like stained glass.
In the deep silence,
every whisper
and shoe scuff
echoed.
I'd perch on the top
and look down
at tiny worshippers,
or stand in the well
and gaze at God's light
suffusing the dome
like milk.

Empty Places

The back alleys of movie theaters,
haunted by dumpsters and the corpses of trash;
long highways in the country so remote
no car or truck's in sight;
parking lots at dawn
deserted but for an attendant up all night;
the vast wheat fields of Iowa seen from a jet
with no sign of man or house at all;
and the vacant homes of Hopper,
baring vulnerable walls
to the cruelties of the sunset:
these places I love,
for I see in them
my own emptiness.

Tower of Babel

We raised it high, proud of our mastery,
our brilliant improvement on our parents'
dark, dusty, old-time ways.
We called it "Progress," metal-and-glass
pile-driver puncturing the clouds.
We believed we were the best, the most
modern, the ones who knew, but when
we reached the top we shouted and shouted
but couldn't comprehend, and then
walls crumbled and down we went
into the black, damp moat from which
we gazed longingly at the vast, lost,
conquering blue.

Naked

At the hot springs, signs blared
"Clothing Optional." A small matter
to take off one's clothes, and not that scary,
so we did. With the first human I passed—

man about forty, paunch, shriveled penis—
I shivered, and not with desire.
Skin to open skin,
we shared something:

intimacy? freedom? God?
I started to stroll the grounds,
seeing and being seen,
my heart escaping through my skin.

I soaked in a bath next to a woman
with huge, firm breasts
I enjoyed without touching.
I walked the paths,

exposing my loins to caressing sun.
Nothing much else:
no orgies, love explosions.
But when we returned to the car,

clothes back on,
we looked at each other
in a new way,
naked, aware,

that lasted almost
till we got home.

After Long Illness

Nice to return and find it still here,
familiar café where I sit in L.A.
Nothing special: tattered coverlets draped
over stained couches, chairs rickety,
nerd leaning intently into a laptop,
cup rings on round, well-worn tables.
I've waited months for this.
I drink my Earl Gray as though
I've never heard of illness,
never known my lungs to ache
or walls to close in like a vise.
No Café aux Deux Magots,
just a place where I'm on vacation,
air balmy, plain teacups encircled
by a nimbus of smoggy light.

My Burg

The fountain in front of Andronico's
supermarket flows crystal pure.
Well-coiffed folks sip lattes,
parade with bags of pluots,
arugula, and petit fours.
Headlines blare Iraq, Katrina,
Darfur—distant rumors.
The greatest concern here's
what fillet to sauté for dinner,
which movie to watch
in the immaculate theater next door.
I read a book and try to stoke
a little fear into my belly,
but it's no use.
The greatest suffering, short of death,
is when the House of Bagel's out of poppy seed.

Rossmoor Twilight

Pines and eucalypti glow rose and salmon.
Maybe there doesn't have to be a meaning.
Maybe these violet iris beds,
azaleas becoming dark and impenetrable,
dim sidewalk with lobelia barely visible in cracks
say everything.
Shall I speak in whispers and half tones?
I traipse along the obscure path,
swallows dipping low above my head.
Then it's fully dark.
The owl hooting in the branches
reminds me it's time to head home.

Addressed to You

Listening to Rachmaninoff in 2007

in memory of my mother

I'm back under the piano, sun washing
my face clean as the music surges.
My infant wrists beat time,
wave after wave of pure passion lifts me
into the light as her fingers make glory
out of dumb wood and wire,
as she made me out of blood and bone . . .
Look, I can see her leaning even now into the keys
ringing out melody, chord and timbre
as my adult heart throbs in unison with hers.

Fossil-Hunting

in memory of my father

You were good at delving into the past.
The great limestone quarry was deserted
but for us. Carefully chipping away
with hammer and chisel, we uncovered
trilobites, brachiopods, fern imprints—
old things safe from the "dangers" of rock 'n' roll,
ducktails, necking.
We came home with a box full,
showed it to visitors with pride:
the philosopher and his admiring son.
Now, a lifetime later,
it sits dusty on my shelf,
while you are history, too.

Manya and Albert

in memory of my parents

Who are these quaint people
with so much power over me?
He's rotund, swings his arms
while walking, tells jokes
that become sarcastic when
he's insecure. She's voluptuous,
doesn't know it, lowers her head
when spoken to, yet screams
obscenities at the repairman
who didn't fix her furnace right.
They were children once,
played with jacks and marbles
on Bronx sidewalks, laughed
at their daddies' jokes.
Now I'm older than they
when I was born,
and feel like comforting them,
suggesting they love themselves
a little more, seeing as,
if I met them for the first time,
I'd probably like them, would say,
let's be friends, Manya and Albert,
hi, my name is Marc.

John

for John Payne

I hadn't heard from you since we were
eight. You were tall, with a high forehead
and so-blue eyes. I felt comfortable
around you, as with the brother
I never had. Once we play-fought
and I fell, gashing my forehead with a scar
I sport still. You leaned over and stroked
my cheek. Then your family moved.
I didn't think we'd ever be in touch again,
but you Googled me this week,
fifty-four years later, wrote kind words,
and sent a photo showing a snow-haired
man with full beard and high forehead.
Many things change, but some don't.

Still Playing

for Don Caplin

We play-boxed like Patterson
and Liston in your parents' home
I dubbed the Smithsonian Institution.
We listened to Les Keiter's recreation
off a ticker tape of the Giants' games
in their first year on the West Coast.
He'd knock a mallet on a block of wood
to simulate bat meeting ball.
I'd laugh when your mother criticized
you and you'd retort, "Nag, nag, nag."
Now we're sixty, pot-bellied, balding,
still friends. You're as funny
as ever. I'm just funny, but we're still
hitting it out of the park.

Enigma

in memory of Alfred Levinson

Elegant-nosed, olive-skinned, taciturn,
curling thin lips into a wry smile,
you taught us balky adolescents
Robert Frost, Shakespeare, Jack London
while scaring us to excel, or fail.
You brushed aside as "nasty gossip"
rumors you'd published poetry and plays.
Never did you speak of wife or kids.
In the hall you prowled on sneakers,
and when I passed you'd nod laconically.
But you said my stories reminded you
of Hemingway and Thomas Wolfe,
thus setting me forth on this journey.
On the last day of tenth grade, Liz Abel and I
followed you all the way home
at a respectful distance, making you laugh.
Forty years later I Google you,
find poetry, a play, three novels,
call your apartment in New York
to find you've died the week before,
elusive to the end.

Provincetown Painter

in memory of Tibor Pataky

Out of place among bronzed beachgoers
and men with willowy walks, pastel tee-shirts,
and cologne, you were old, tall and gangly
and slashed lurid pigment on canvas,
not caring what people thought.
Your forms were writhing parabola and flash.
Once in a while you'd let me—
fourteen, fifteen, sixteen,
just starting to write poems and date girls—
take a peek at a mature man's passions
splayed across a twelve-foot wall.
They said you and your wife fought,
that you were "crazy."
To me you were sweet as a father, and encouraging,
you whose colors, turbulent and vibrant,
are hung across the skies of my youth.

Music Professor

in memory of Peter Gram Swing

I thought you English with your cultured
accent, your way of calling us puling
undergraduates "Mister" and "Miss,"
your taste for French expressions, and for song,
especially. You taught us
Figaro, Tristan, and the *B Minor Mass,*
your torso rocking backward and forward
as you lectured on Brahms and Debussy,
your eyes filling with tears during the
adagio of the *Brandenburg* Number 1.
Hearing, years later, you'd died,
I couldn't believe such energy, such feeling
could go. But I want to think
you're with your immortals now,
playing arias, cantatas.

Son House

You toiled out onto the stage,
guitar in one hand, white handkerchief
in the other. You said, "I'se jes' an ole
man, and I cain't play the geetar like
I use' to, but I'se gonna try."
You drew out steel-gray notes
that rose and flew off like
mourning doves into the clouds.
You'd pulled your feet from the mud
of Mississippi to come up
to our white-bread campus and teach
us something we couldn't learn in class.
Now you're in those clouds,
and I'm here trying to emulate your voice.
I'm just an old man, and I can't sing
like I used to, but I'se gonna try.

Côte-d'Or Visit

for David Mus

I visited you where walls were the color
of clay and roof tiles orange
and grapevines shaded you and Wendy
from summer heat your fine nose
and white parchment skin unchanged
and your shelves of course filled
with poetry books and we spoke
of Baudelaire Villon *le beau pays*
and then the sun slowly set
and I went away an American
in love with France earthen walls
poetry and you who remained

Monsieur Fillet

We knocked on your door in desperation
in the narrow treeless street
"Marcel Fillet *Agent Immobilier*"
and you clanked out from the back room
cane and prosthesis striking the floor
head bald as a buzzard's
you volunteered you lost your leg in Algeria
and as you heard we couldn't
find an apartment your eyes softened
you rose and declared, *"N'ayez pas peur.*
Je vous trouverai un appartement!"
and three days later you handed us the keys
to 13, rue du Grenier à Sel
and in the winter you had us over for dinner
you and your wife and two curly-haired daughters
and before we left Orléans we thanked you
and your eyes softened again
where are you Marcel Fillet
still banging your leg
still finding strangers homes?

Bipsy

in memory of Elizabeth Hansen

I've chosen to go to a different teahouse today
because Bipsy is dead
and things don't make sense.
She was my favorite neighbor,
tending hydrangeas and lantanas,
white hair sticking from beneath
wide-brimmed hat, like some eccentric
Englishwoman on a TV mystery,
keen-eyed, who divulges to the detective
the whole solution
before he's even started thinking.
It turns out she had cancer,
but she didn't mention that.
I never stepped into her house,
or she into mine, though she invited me
(always too busy) many times.
We could have sipped tea together,
discussed Virginia Woolf.
Now her car's here, her house all
freshly painted, shades down . . .
Her face is imprinted on my mind.
Her hair gleams.
I sip some First Flush Darjeeling—
I wonder whether she would have liked it—
and think about how soon
I'll have to thrust thoughts of Bipsy away,
make dinner, go to class,
while her Jetta sits there in her driveway,
blue and alone, all alone.

Old Man Smoking

Fingers curled around a cigarette,
he slouches in his chair.
His eyes are brown islands
in a sea of white.
I'm never sure if he'll
ask me for spare change,
or tell me some great truth.
I always see him in this café,
too old to be earning money,
too beset by life's demands
to do more than sit, sprawl,
and exchange soulful glances with me,
who might be his son,
his brother,
or his younger self.

Migrant

for Tony Z

You've worked a lifetime, proud of your hands
for having built your adopted country
as if it were your own. Do they belong to you,
Tony, "fag," "spic," the millions
you've stashed away over sixty years
bringing you nothing more than my poor company,
a consolation no doubt but no substitute
for family, old friends? You show
me your apartment, but I'm in a hurry
to carry out a hundred errands
and don't know if I want to meet again,
the serendipity of the doctor's waiting room
behind us. What can you tell me, Tony,
except with your scarred hand that shakes mine
as we part, then falls to your side
like a limp fish, alive, still breathing?

Two Intellectuals in a Coffeehouse

One has a pubic beard
and a wen on his ear,
the other a voice like a wire
and stiff hands.
They speak of the moral imperative,
the keenness of Occam's razor,
how feeble God is.
They leave nothing unturned.
What do they care about the clam's soft belly,
what difference does the
heart of the artichoke make to them,
when will they
stop talking?

Buddy, My Dog for a Week

I – DURING THE WEEK

I lie curled in bed, knees to belly,
like you, Buddy.
I flop down on chairs.
Yawning, I bare incisors.
I gulp down big chunks of beef
with sauce.
Every once in a while
I sigh without warning.
I'm trying to be like you
because then you'll stay with me forever—
each breath I take,
each heartbeat matching yours.

II – AFTER THE WEEK

You taught me how to sniff the breeze
for pine sap and rank moss,
gape at the mad rush of a squirrel up a trunk,
hear goldfinches click branches
with tin feet,
thrill to winter sun turning the sky
blue with joy,
relish beef as though it were
my last meal,
love with tongue and eye,
be in the world and of the world,
and then you taught me to let go.

Keep On

That snow-haired, bespectacled old man
with the round, pink face and flat nose
and the red-and-green plaid shirt
sipping tea in the teahouse
seems to me as heroic as a fireman on 9/11,
a lineman facing a blitz,
or a hot air balloonist taking off for Martinique.
Look at how his thoughtful smile
softens the deep lines around his mouth,
how his leaning elbows cannily
ease the heavy weight from his upper back,
how his faint blue eyes say
Keep on, keep on, keep on.
I'd like to shake his hand,
hear some helpful words,
or warm myself at his smile
but he's a stranger.
I can't suck up his strength.
I can only try to be a bit like him.

The Return

for David

Things are looking up.
Our ducks are back.
Who would have thought it:
a whole year and no sign—
flown to Brazil, Belize?—
but here they are,
green-headed mallard
and his speckled brown wife
looking up at our screen door again,
quacking. We toss out
cracked corn, which they snap up
with leathery bills.
Later we catch them peering
in from the atrium
with velvet brown eyes
like yours.
Will they stay now?
Do they love us?

Making Love

Making Love by
Thousand Islands Lake, 1970

Our limbs burned, wild as the billion
worlds flaring crazily in chilled air,
drifting lake mist
heightening every sense.
I knew your hips and breasts,
your warm mound as precisely
as algebraic equations or the war in Vietnam.
Your hair smelled like goldenrod,
your cunt felt like moss,
while Mount Ritter reigned above us,
granitic, unchanging.
A shooting star plummeted,
blazing as it died.
After three months of love,
and two weeks among the peaks,
how could I know this would be
our last night together,
that in a few days you'd leave me?
In the morning we hiked to the trailhead,
turned, and silently said goodbye
to the mountains, the lupine, everything.

Remember?

I remember how pink you looked
in your White Duck dress, how the rabbi
guided my hand writing my Hebrew name
(you didn't need his help),
how the glass at first wouldn't break
when I stomped on it, how you
almost fainted as we said our vows,
the finger food, strawberry shortcake, Chardonnay,
folk guitarist, dancing, laughter
rising higher and higher as spirits took off . . .

You may reject this now, but I don't;
I embrace it as one might a lost child,
or moth struggling to fly up and out.
Remember how we did our brow-to-brow
to look cross-eyed at one another
after all the others had left?
People who do things like that don't forget,
do they? I still like to think
of your straight nose, how you'd blush
when laughing, or your skill
at getting plants to grow.
And you—does my face float pleasantly
before you ever, does my voice
come to you in dreams, does my name
evoke anything but bitterness and scorn?

Over

Sun shines wan through dusty café windows
onto stained tables and weathered, peeling chairs.
Cups are half-drained, ashtrays full,
newspapers scattered over tables and floor.
Our love is a spot of sunshine
the busboy has suddenly swept away.

Young Women in a Teahouse

These teenagers can't stop giggling:
one with kittenish mouth, the other
raven-tressed with green-gold eyes.
No comic image on a screen,
nothing funny on the stereo,
no one telling jokes.
These girls teach me as much
as any ancient monk, the *Gita,*
or *Being and Time.* I will
follow them down their path of
mirth and bliss as far as it leads,
through suffering and pain
if necessary—to death,
if it comes to that.

Burden

My friend Larry's pee-pee was fat as a worm
but, when we played, became a rocket ship.
I was too young to know what I was,
but when Dick Harris laughed about "fags"
in fifth-grade recess, I cringed.
I wouldn't mention this to anyone
until I was thirty-five years old.
It was my secret and Larry's,
hidden from my wife, friends,
parents, myself.
I carried it like a burden through PE class,
final exams, France, Israel,
frugalities and fellowships.
I can feel it even now, weighing me down
like a sack of rocks,
laughing at me across the years.

Castro Morning

After getting fucked deep in night
and sleeping royally,
I have the Sunday morning streets to myself,
sun glancing off them like a high-five,
my asshole tingling like a satisfied mouse,
the coffeehouse vacant
but for one sharp-eyed man
with whom I share a complicit smile.

Sonnet

Atop the crenellated air we fucked
like cranes, simulating conjunctions
of spidery hoarfrost or prepositions
plummeting to the ground. "Howdy"
wasn't the approach, I'm a cinch
to be uncomfortable at the least,
at the most to buy thirty lavender
soaps to form the crux of our friendship.
No barriers flummoxed our thirst
to dangle pendulous organs at midnight.
Your swimming-hole is difficult and tough
yet sweet as the small eye of a quail,
in the end milk floats on the rippling foam
of a long and very wooly word.

Young Man

He enters the teahouse: blond
straw-matted hair, eyes
lobelia blue, chick down
on his cheeks,
rocky shoulders meant to be held
by someone he loves.
If I were a girl he would be
alert, taut, ready to perform
whatever dance the moment cried for
but, since I'm not, his gaze
is relaxed, a bit diffuse,
that of a boy much younger,
a child, almost.
When he catches me desiring him
everything will change—he'll
tense up, and distaste and fear
will fill his eyes—
I know that expression.
But the moment hasn't come yet
so I look while I can.

Perfection

He was ideal: yellow hair,
snail-like nose, cornflower eyes.
But he performed sex for cash,
so when I approached him I expected
sleaze, was surprised by
his generous embrace, kind voice—
the sort of thing that
happens in a dream,
which is exactly what this
turned out to be.

Tawny

That fellow with the hair
and all the tawny skin
could be the singing subject
for echoing cherubim.
No gainsaying bright eyes,
moist cheeks and arms
that induce long sighs
from burning lips,
but he looks mean,
and there's no sense
in wasting dream
on mindless prurience.

Happiness

in memory of Daniel Deskins

He hung them on all his walls:
pastels of penises, one a volcano
spitting milky spume, another a pine
thrusting furious phloem into air, a third
a skyscraper spreading joy
all over a mopey city, spurting
fountains, obelisks, cattails, silos,
his obsession making him grin with delight
as he showed them to me, ecstasy
become his hourly preoccupation,
his yardstick for value, his sense of meaning,
and that night he pampered my penis
as we lay in bed, treated it
as something holy, and so I learned from him
how to worship the life of happiness
day and night.

Seven Sumo Wrestlers in the Ocean

after a photograph

We float in breakers,
which carry us,
seven portly men
with a common practice.
Who says we're fat?
Who claims we're mean?
We're strong, naked,
happy, wanting only
to link in lightness,
clasp hands in fun.
Say hey!
Seven Sumo wrestlers
with a good word:
cheer us!
Love us!
Watch us swim!

Eternity

for David

I protected your nipples, your wrists
in the darkness and I thought,
This is where I was meant to be,
and,
This is where I have always been,
and,
This is where I will always be,
and you shifted slightly
and before I knew it
the sun shone fiery on the window
and the stars were gone.

Notes

22 Crescent Road: In my hometown of Larchmont, Westchester County, New York.

Kibbutz Mizra: In the Jezreel Valley of northern Israel.

Israeli Cockroaches: The Kinneret is the Israeli name for what we call the Sea of Galilee.

Particulars: The Crum is a river that flows through the campus of Swarthmore College, where I was an undergraduate.

In a Music Store: Salif Keita is a Malian singer, Matti Caspi an Israeli one. Bix is Bix Beiderbecke, the great jazz cornet player of the 1920s.

Rossmoor Twilight: Rossmoor is the Contra Costa County, California, retirement community in which I live.

In Memoriam Alfred Levinson: Alfred Levinson, my tenth grade English teacher in Mamaroneck High School, Mamaroneck, New York, was the author of three books of poetry—*Cauldron* (James A. Decker, 1948), *Paris, Lost and Found* (Tribune Internationale de Poésie, 1968), and *Travelogs* (Signford, 1981), a trilogy of novels entitled *Fish Tales* (Oracle Press, 1984), and numerous other books.

Provincetown Painter: Tibor Pataky was a Hungarian-born Abstract Expressionist who spent summers in the nineteen fifties, as my parents and I did, in Provincetown, Massachusetts.

Music Professor: Peter Gram Swing was Chairman of the Music Department at Swarthmore College in the nineteen sixties.

Son House: A great Mississippi Delta blues singer, born 1902, died 1988. I heard him perform at Swarthmore College in 1965.

Côte-d'Or Visit: David Mus is an American-born American and French poet who taught French literature at Swarthmore in the sixties and moved to the hamlet of Jailly-les-Moulins in the Côte-d'Or region of Burgundy in 1965. He is the author of many books of poetry and prose in English and French, including *La Poétique de Francois Villon* (Armand Colin, 1967), *Wall to Wall Speaks* (Princeton University Press, 1988), *D'un accord/Double stopping* (Ulysse, Fin de Siècle, 1991) and *Qu'alors on ne se souviendra plus de la mer Rouge* (Ragage, 2005).

Monsieur Fillet: 13, rue du Grenier à Sel was my ex-wife's and my address in Orléans, France during the academic year of 1977-1978 when I taught English language and American literature at the Université d'Orléans on a Fulbright lectureship. *"N'ayez pas peur,/Je vous trouverai un appartement!":* "Never fear, I will find you an apartment!"

Making Love by Thousand Islands Lake, 1970: Thousand Islands Lake is in the Minaret Peaks of the Sierra Nevada in central California.

Remember?: White Duck was a clothing store, now defunct, in Berkeley.

About the Author

Marc Elihu Hofstadter was born in New York City in 1945. He received his B.A. degree in French Literature from Swarthmore College in 1967, and his Ph.D. in Literature from the University of California at Santa Cruz in 1975. From 1977 to 1978 he was Fulbright Lecturer in American Literature and English Language at the Université d'Orléans, and in 1978 and 1979 he taught American literature at Tel Aviv University. In 1980 he obtained his Master of Library and Information Studies degree from the University of California at Berkeley and, from 1982 to 2005, served as the librarian of the City of San Francisco's transit agency. He has published three previous volumes of poetry, *House of Peace* (Mother's Hen Press, 1999), *Visions* (Scarlet Tanager Books, 2001), and *Shark's Tooth* (Regent Press, 2006), and his poems, translations, and essays have appeared in over sixty magazines and in the anthology of writings about tea, *Steeped*. Hofstadter won the Whetstone (Barrington Writers Workshop) Poetry Prize for 2004. He is a member of one of the United States' leading intellectual families. His uncle Robert Hofstadter won the Nobel Prize in physics, his cousins Douglas and Richard Hofstadter were both awarded the Pulitzer Prize, his father Albert Hofstadter was an acclaimed philosopher, his mother Manya Huber an award-winning concert pianist, and his uncle Samuel Huber a noted painter. Hofstadter lives in Walnut Creek, California with his partner, the artist David Zurlin.

Also from Scarlet Tanager Books

Bone Strings by Anne Coray
    poetry, 80 pages, $15.00

Wild One by Lucille Lang Day
    poetry, 100 pages, $12.95

The "Fallen Western Star" Wars: A Debate About Literary California, edited by Jack Foley
    essays, 88 pages, $14.00

Catching the Bullet & Other Stories by Daniel Hawkes
    fiction, 64 pages, $12.95

Visions: Paintings Seen Through the Optic of Poetry by Marc Elihu Hofstadter
    poetry, 72 pages, $16.00

Embrace by Risa Kaparo
    poetry, 70 pages, $14.00

red clay is talking by Naomi Ruth Lowinsky
    poetry, 142 pages, $ 14.95

crimes of the dreamer by Naomi Ruth Lowinsky
    poetry, 82 pages, $16.00

The Number Before Infinity by Zack Rogow
    poetry, 72 pages, $16.00

Everything Irish by Judy Wells
    poetry, 112 pages, $12.95

Call Home by Judy Wells
    poetry, 92 pages, $15.00

Printed in the United States
204642BV00001B/190-579/P